Shropshire Libraries	
75182	
PETERS	23-Mar-2020
J531	£12.99

Theme Park Science

FORCES at the THEME PARK

by Tammy Enz

raintree
a Capstone company — publishers for children

Raintree is an imprint of Capstone Global Library Limited, a company incorporated in England and Wales having its registered office at 264 Banbury Road, Oxford, OX2 7DY – Registered company number: 6695582

www.raintree.co.uk
myorders@raintree.co.uk

Text © Capstone Global Library Limited 2020
The moral rights of the proprietor have been asserted.

All rights reserved. No part of this publication may be reproduced in any form or by any means (including photocopying or storing it in any medium by electronic means and whether or not transiently or incidentally to some other use of this publication) without the written permission of the copyright owner, except in accordance with the provisions of the Copyright, Designs and Patents Act 1988 or under the terms of a licence issued by the Copyright Licensing Agency, Barnard's Inn, 86 Fetter Lane, London, EC4A 1EN (www.cla.co.uk). Applications for the copyright owner's written permission should be addressed to the publisher.

Edited by Carrie Braulick Sheely
Designed by Tracy McCabe
Original illustrations © Capstone Global Library Limited 2020
Picture research by Eric Gohl
Production by Kathy McColley
Originated by Capstone Global Library Ltd
Printed and bound in India

978 1 4747 8512 9 (hardback)
978 1 4747 8516 7 (paperback)

British Library Cataloguing in Publication Data
A full catalogue record for this book is available from the British Library.

Acknowledgements
We would like to thank the following for permission to reproduce photographs: Alamy: Angie Knost, 21, Charles de Candolle, 17, Herb Quick, 1 (background), 7, Ryan McGinnis, 6; iStockphoto: Denise Bernadette, back cover (background), 5, kali9, 8, Nikada, 23; Newscom/ZUMA Press: Paul Rodriguez, 9, Richard Lautens, 29; Shutterstock: Abai Bekenov, 19, anek. soowannaphoom, 27, Eric Broder Van Dyke, 15, i-m-a-g-e, cover (top), Jacob Lund, 25, Krylovochka, cover (bottom), 1 (bottom), Racheal Grazias, 13; Wikimedia: WillMcC, 11. Design elements: Shutterstock.

Every effort has been made to contact copyright holders of material reproduced in this book. Any omissions will be rectified in subsequent printings if notice is given to the publisher.

All the internet addresses (URLs) given in this book were valid at the time of going to press. However, due to the dynamic nature of the internet, some addresses may have changed, or sites may have changed or ceased to exist since publication. While the author and publisher regret any inconvenience this may cause readers, no responsibility for any such changes can be accepted by either the author or the publisher.

CONTENTS

Chapter 1
The forces of fun 4

Chapter 2
Pushing and pulling from near and far 6

Chapter 3
Get a grip with gravity 12

Chapter 4
The spin on centripetal force...............20

Chapter 5
More forces....................................24

Glossary..30
Comprehension questions 31
Find out more..................................31
Index...32

CHAPTER 1
THE FORCES OF FUN

Scream at the top of your voice as you zoom through a loop on a white-knuckle roller coaster ride. Feel your stomach flutter as the Ferris wheel cranks its way to the top. Hold on as the drop tower makes its plunge. What do these thrills all have in common? They all rely on forces for fantastic fun!

What is a force? A force is simply a pull or a push on an object. Forces make things move, slow down, speed up, stay in place or change shape. A force pulls roller coaster cars up. Another force pulls them down. A force stops the seats spinning off a twirling ride. Another force holds you up when you flop down on a bench. Even when you're sitting still, forces are at work.

As a roller coaster speeds through a loop, a force keeps it going in a circular motion.

Without forces a theme park would be very dull. What are you waiting for? Take a deep breath. Then get ready for a tour of theme park forces that push, pull and make your pulse pound.

FACT:
Disney theme parks are the most popular in the world. The Magic Kingdom in Florida, USA, attracts the most visitors.

CHAPTER 2

PUSHING AND PULLING FROM NEAR AND FAR

Contact force

Grab your friend's hand and pull her to the games. You've just applied a force – a **contact force**. A contact force is easy to see. It is pushing or pulling directly on something as two objects touch.

You'll see a big show of contact force when you try out the Test your strength game. In this game, you slam a mallet down on a pad. It pushes a puck up a tower. When you lift that mallet over your head and slam it down, you are using a powerful pushing force. Did the bell ring at the top of the tower? Well done! That's another contact force as the puck hits the bell.

A hard slam with a mallet forces the puck up a tower in the Test your strength game.

Compressed air in contact with the drop tower can send it skywards.

Most theme park rides need a contact force to get them going. A chain wrapped around a gear slowly pulls roller-coaster cars up the first big hill. In the drop tower ride, the force of **compressed air** pushes the ride up.

contact force direct push or pull on or off something in which the two objects are touching

compressed air air under pressure greater than that of the atmosphere

Buoyant force

Do you like the lazy river ride? Have you ever wondered why you can happily float down the river in your tube? What type of force holds you up? This force is called buoyant force. Buoyant force is a contact force that pushes directly on your tube.

Whether an object floats depends on the object's weight and how much water is moved away (displaced). The water pushes up on an object with a force equal to the weight of the water displaced. If the weight of the object is less than the weight of the water displaced, it will float. Your tube is mostly made of air. It has low **density**. Its light weight helps it easily float. But if you drop your phone into the water, it sinks. Your phone weighs more than the water it displaces.

Lightweight tubes easily float down the lazy river.

Doughnuts rise to the top of the oil as they become less dense.

You might gobble up a bag of mini doughnuts at the theme park. But have you ever wondered how these deep-fried delicious treats came to be? Buoyant force is at work here too. Raw doughnut dough sinks to the bottom of the hot oil when it is first dropped in. But as the doughnut cooks, air pockets expand inside it. They make the doughnut less dense and it rises to float on the oil.

SINK OR FLOAT?

How much an object's surface area touches the water also affects its buoyancy. When you are upright in water, you tend to sink. If you lie on your back, you have a better chance of floating. More of your body touches the water's surface.

density relationship of an object's mass (material it contains) to its volume (amount of space it takes up)

Electromagnetic force

Not all forces push or pull by making contact. Some powerful forces work from a distance.

Have you ever played with magnets? All around a magnet is an invisible force called a magnetic field. You can't see it, but you know it's there, because the magnet can attract some metal objects.

Magnets can be really useful at a theme park. A type of magnet called an electromagnet uses electricity to create **electromagnetic force**. An electromagnet is different from the sort of magnet you use on your fridge. An electromagnet has wire between the two ends (poles). The wire wraps around a metal core. A power source, such as a battery, supplies electricity to make a current. The current flows through the wire. This creates a magnetic field around the core. The electromagnet loses power when the flow of electricity stops. It then no longer has a magnetic field. An ordinary magnet always has a magnetic field.

Some roller coasters, drop towers and other types of rides use electromagnetic force in their braking systems. Magnets on the moving cars cause electrical currents as they move past fins that are **conductive**. A magnetic force is created. It is strong enough to stop speeding rides.

conductive allowing heat, electricity or sound to easily travel through

electromagnetic force force caused by a magnetic field created by electric currents

The fins for electromagnetic braking systems are often along the side of a roller coaster track.

CHAPTER 3

GET A GRIP WITH GRAVITY

Magnetic forces aren't the only forces that work at a distance. The scariest part of a roller coaster might be that slow ride up the first hill. Why is that? Because everybody knows what comes next – the death-defying ride back down. Roller coaster cars don't have an engine to power them along the track. Once they are lifted up that first big hill, a force of nature takes over.

What type of amazing force makes that possible? It's a force that affects you every day, but one you probably don't think about a lot. It's **gravity**! Gravity is the force that pulls everything on our planet towards the centre of Earth.

Gravity is at work on many rides. You can bet the **pendulum** ride relies on gravity. Each time you swing up, gravity pulls you back down.

Gravity pulls roller coaster cars down the first big hill.

gravity force that pulls objects down towards the centre of Earth

pendulum weight that hangs from a fixed point and swings back and forth freely using the force of gravity

G-force

Have you noticed that near the top of the swinging pendulum ride you feel like you're floating? This feeling is called weightlessness. Then when you're near the bottom, you feel really heavy. A force causes these sensations.

When something falls, it doesn't fall at an even speed. It speeds up. This change in speed is called acceleration. The force caused by this acceleration is called gravity force, also known as **g-force**. Standing still we always feel 1 g-force (1 g) on our bodies. This g-force gives us weight.

But some rides really mess up the g-force we feel. You can feel almost 4 g at the bottom of some roller coaster loops or pendulum rides. At the bottom of a ride you feel the acceleration of the moving ride plus the acceleration from gravity. As you accelerate down, your seat pushes up with the same amount of force. The force you feel from your seat makes you feel four times heavier than usual.

g-force force of gravity or acceleration on a moving object

DANGEROUS POSITIVE G-FORCE

The human body can safely travel at any speed – even millions of kilometres per hour! But it has to take its time getting to high speeds. Heavy accelerations cause you to be pushed back into your seat. Your blood rushes to your feet. This action causes a lack of oxygen in the brain. Accelerations between 4 and 8 g can cause you to faint. Even higher g-force can cause death. Pilots often experience high g-force. They need special training, clothing and breathing techniques to survive these forces.

Riders feel weightless as a pendulum reaches its top height.

Weightlessness

If loading up on g-force makes you feel like a tonne of bricks, feeling less g-force can get your stomach rolling. As you begin dropping from the top of the pendulum ride or the drop tower, you feel breathless – and weightless! But why? Gravity is still at work, pulling you down. But it's also pulling your seat down at the same time. You and the seat are both in free fall. As both you and your seat are falling at the same time, your seat is not pressing on you. Because you don't feel your seat pressing on you, you feel weightless. At the top of the pendulum, you are feeling less than 1 g. This is the same feeling you get if you miss a step when going down stairs. As you tumble, you feel weightless until your foot touches another stair.

As you speed downwards on the drop tower, both you and your seat are in free fall.

DANGEROUS NEGATIVE G-FORCE

When you feel negative g-force, your body is travelling faster than your blood moves inside you. It causes blood to pool in your head. Negative g-force can be even more dangerous than positive g-force. No human can withstand between −2 and −3 g without fainting. Luckily, theme park rides never get close to that.

Normal force

Gravity is always pulling on us. But there are forces working against gravity too.

What happens when you sit down on a park bench after an exhausting day of rides? Something stops gravity from pulling you all the way down. It's the force of the bench pushing you back up. This force is called a **normal force**. As long as the normal force and the gravity force are equal (balanced), you can happily sit still on the bench eating your candyfloss. When you lean against a wall or push against your safety strap, normal force balances your applied force.

But what happens if the forces aren't balanced? What if you sit down on a bench that's got a wobbly leg? Now the bench might not be able to provide a normal force to balance out gravity. Gravity might win out and you'll end up on the ground. Ouch!

---

normal force contact force pushing back against an equal applied force

As you sit on a bench, normal force pushes up on you.

ELECTROSTATIC FORCE

Want a real charge at the theme park? Try rubbing a balloon against your hair. Then touch the balloon to a metal gate at the park to see some sparks fly. By rubbing the balloon against your hair, you created an electric charge, which is needed to make **electrostatic force**. Metal is a conductive material. That means electricity flows easily through it. When you touch the charged balloon to metal, the electric charges rush to the metal. That's what creates the sparks!

electrostatic force force caused by an electric charge

CHAPTER 4
THE SPIN ON CENTRIPETAL FORCE

Have you ever let go of a roundabout in the park when spinning very fast? You probably flew off. Objects that are being spun around in a circle try to move outwards in a straight line. A force keeps them spinning in a circular path. This force is called **centripetal force**. It pulls towards the centre of a circle.

You'd fly off spinning theme park rides without centripetal force. The base of a merry-go-round and the metal arms of spinning rides supply this force. As long as you hold on to your horse or stay strapped in your seat, centripetal force will keep you on the ride.

What about the rotor ride? In this spinning ride, there is nothing to hold to keep you connected to the centre. But the walls of the ride do the job. They force you towards the centre of the circle as the spinning cylinder forces you outwards. The ride spins at just the right speed to keep you pinned to the wall.

> **centripetal force** force that pulls spinning objects to the centre of a circle

The walls keep you on the rotor ride as it spins.

Centripetal force also helps to keep you in your seat as you zip through a roller coaster loop. At the very top, gravity tries to bring you down. But centripetal force overcomes it, keeping you turning.

FACT:
Centrifugal force is the force that works against centripetal force. It's what pulls you away from the centre of a spinning circle.

Tension force

Swinging rides don't have walls or arms to keep you moving in a circle. Something else provides centripetal force. The chains or ropes that hold your seat to the centre of the circle provide it.

When the chain is stretched tight as the ride spins, it pulls your seat towards the centre of the circle. It forces you to keep swinging instead of spinning off. A chain or rope that is pulled tightly is in tension. It is supplying a **tension force**.

Have you ever noticed how a rope or a chain can be easily bent or pushed when hanging loosely? But when it is pulled it becomes very strong. That's tension force at work. Tension force is strong enough to hold you and your seat as you swing.

---

tension force pulling force in a rope, chain or wire

There is tension force in the chains on the swing ride.

CHAPTER 5
MORE FORCES

Air resistance

Imagine you're hurtling down the first big hill of a roller coaster. Your hands are in the air. You are screaming with all your might. Suddenly you feel your hair lifting away from your head. You know gravity is pulling you down. But what is pulling your hair up and away? This force is called **air resistance**.

Air resistance is the force you feel when you move through air. It might seem like air is made of nothing. But it is made of gases. Moving through air is similar to moving through water. The faster you move through air, the more it pushes back. Your lightweight hair can't force its way through air the way your body can. It gets pushed up and away.

The shape of an object affects how easily it moves through air. Sleek, pointed objects cut through air more easily. Notice the shape of the dart you use at the balloon dart game. Its smooth design and fins help it to cut through air.

The faster you go on a roller coaster, the more air pushes against you.

air resistance force that resists movement as an object passes through air

25

Friction

You're hurrying to the next ride when you slip and fall. Which force let you down? An unexpected decrease in **friction** caused you to lose your balance and fall. You depend on friction to help you walk safely without falling.

Friction is a force between two objects as they move against each other. Designers may try to reduce friction on some rides to make them faster and more fun. But in other places around the park, they try to increase friction.

Roller coaster rails are very smooth so that friction won't slow the ride. The waterslide is also smooth and slippery. It allows you smooth sailing to the bottom of the ride.

But have a look at some of the gritty pads on the platforms as you find your seat on a ride. These rough surfaces grip your feet. The friction stops you slipping.

---

friction force caused by objects rubbing together

Friction can also be helpful to slow down and stop rides. Ferris wheels and some roller coasters have friction brakes. Rubber clamps grab moving parts of the rides and friction force stops the rides.

The stream of water running down a waterslide also helps to reduce friction.

FACT
When two objects rub together, the friction causes heat. With enough friction, the heat can start a fire. Rubbing two bits of wood together can cause a spark to start a campfire.

Spring force

No day at the park is complete without taking in a show. How about watching the human cannonball? You'll be amazed as a huge cannon flings a person into a net.

What force is powerful enough for this feat? Spring force can do the trick! Spring force comes from a **compressed** or stretched spring. The spring goes back to its natural state when released. In the past, cannons used real springs. Some modern cannons use bungee cords. The bungee cord still acts like a spring. The strong force flings the person out of the cannon. The person can travel at more than 97 kilometres (60 miles) per hour!

You might also see spring force at work in the acrobatics show. What happens when a performer jumps on the trampoline? She stretches the springs attached to the fabric. When they spring back, she flies into the air!

---

compress press or squeeze together

Human cannonballs can fly more than 23 metres (75 feet) in the air.

Theme parks are a thrill a minute. Enjoy all the excitement. But don't forget to thank forces for their part in making your day unforgettable!

FACT:
Some cannons use compressed air instead of bungee cords to push out the performer.

GLOSSARY

air resistance force that resists movement as an object passes through air

centripetal force force that pulls spinning objects to the centre of a circle

compress press or squeeze together

compressed air air under pressure greater than that of the atmosphere

conductive allowing heat, electricity or sound to easily travel through

contact force direct push or pull on something in which the two objects are touching

density relationship of an object's mass (material it contains) to its volume (amount of space it takes up)

electromagnetic force force caused by a magnetic field created by electric currents

electrostatic force force caused by electric charge

friction force caused by objects rubbing together

g-force force of gravity or acceleration on a moving object

gravity force that pulls objects down towards the centre of Earth

normal force contact force pushing back against an equal applied force

pendulum weight that hangs from a fixed point and swings back and forth freely using the force of gravity

tension force pulling force in a rope, chain or wire

COMPREHENSION QUESTIONS

1. When objects spin in a circular motion, centripetal force is at work. Can you think of everyday actions that involve centripetal force? What would happen if centrifugal force took over during the movement?

2. If you drop a heavy ball and a feather from the top of the Ferris wheel, the feather takes longer to hit the ground. Why do you think this happens? Use reference books or the internet to help explain your answer.

3. When going down the waterslide, you brace your feet against the sides of the slide to slow down. What force are you using?

FIND OUT MORE

BOOKS

Ride that Rollercoaster: Forces in an Amusement Park (Feel the Force), Louise and Richard Spilsbury (Raintree, 2016)

Science Experiments: Loads of Explosively Fun Activities You Can Do!, Robert Winston (DK Children, 2011)

When Forces and Motion Collide, Chris Oxlade (Raintree, 2017)

WEBSITES

www.bbc.co.uk/bitesize/articles/zptckqt
Learn more about different types of forces.

www.dkfindout.com/uk/science/forces-and-motion/what-is-force
Find out more about forces.

INDEX

air resistance 24

buoyant force 8–9

centrifugal force 21
centripetal force 20–21, 22
compressed air 7, 29
contact forces 6–7, 8

density 8, 9
drop towers 4, 7, 11, 16

electromagnetic force 10–11
electromagnets 10–11
electrostatic force 19

friction 26–27

g-forces 14, 15, 16, 17
gravity 12, 14, 16, 18, 21, 24

normal force 18

pendulum 12, 14, 16

roller coasters 4, 5, 7, 11, 12, 13, 14, 21, 24, 25, 27
rotor ride 20

spring force 28

tension force 22
Test your strength game 6

weightlessness 14, 16